·········· FIVESTARMAN ··········
FIELD GUIDE
and
45-DAY CHALLENGE

······································

★ FIVESTARMAN™

THIS FIELD GUIDE IS THE PROPERTY OF:

....

PERTINENT COORDINATES:

....
....
....
....
....

Fivestarman
82 Plantation Pointe
Fairhope, AL 36532
Fivestarman.com

★FIVESTARMAN™

THE FIVE PASSIONS OF AUTHENTIC MANHOOD

ADVENTUROUS
A Fivestarman is adventurous. Seeking new challenges with passion and determination, encouraging others to join in.

ENTREPRENEURIAL
A Fivestarman is entrepreneurial. Passionate in the discovery of new ideas that provide new sources of income, embracing and building on the entrepreneurial spirit.

GALLANT
A Fivestarman is gallant. Courageous in battle, fighting passionately to defend the weak and less fortunate. He is gallant in his respect of women and heroic in his defense of children.

FAITHFUL
A Fivestarman is faithful. Unwavering in the truths he holds dear, a Fivestarman understands that true freedom comes when he is submitted to Godly authority.

PHILANTHROPIC
A Fivestarman is philanthropic. Legendary in his desire to live beyond his own interests, ever ready to champion a worthy cause, and willing to respond with resources and action.

★FIVESTARMAN

Be sure to visit the online version of the
Fivestarman 45-Day Challenge at

CHALLENGE.FIVESTARMAN.COM

Many of the daily challenges and tips are
more fully explored online and you'll have the
opportunity to share your thoughts and stories
with fellow like-minded men.

I want to welcome you to the Challenge – the Authentic Manhood Challenge. This is your opportunity to embrace and process the Five Passions of Authentic Manhood into your life.

Over the next 45 days you will draw upon deep rivers of authentic manhood and awaken passions that reside within you. Make no mistake – this isn't a program to make you something that you are not but rather to reveal the original intent of what God made you to be.

The Field Guide will kick start your day as you work through and embrace the challenges and ideals set forth. You will shake off those things that hinder you and press toward the mark of a higher calling in your life.

You may be tempted to read this guide as you would a typical book, reading from beginning to end and calling it done, but I encourage you to focus fully on each day's challenge and intent and use it as a daily roadmap as you chart your course to greatness.

So get ready, dig deep, and work hard. It won't be easy. You will want to quit. It's a decision that you must make to step up and be an authentic man.

–Neil Kennedy

HERE'S HOW THE GUIDE WORKS

PRECEPT

Each day we will focus on one of the five passions of authentic manhood. We begin with a Precept. A precept is an established and foundational truth that is unchangeable, irrevocable, and eternal.

PRINCIPLE

We will then interpret the precept into a Principle. A principle gives us clear understanding for the universal nature of the precept. We will embolden the principle so that it is easily recognized.

PRACTICE

We then put the principle into Practice. We must apply the principle into our lives. We will give you achievable steps to do so.

TODAY'S CHALLENGE

This may seem simple at times, at other times it may seem impossible. You should make every effort to take the spirit of the challenge and implement it. If you do, you will be amazed at the results you achieve over the period of just 45 days.

ACTION STEPS

Finally, you should record your Action Steps. The steps of a good man are order by the Lord (Psalm 37:23). Write down your thoughts, actions, even your committal prayers for this Challenge.

LET'S GET GOING

> *"I run straight to the goal with purpose in every step!"*
> 1 Corinthians 9:26

The Challenge is more than a self-help program. **This is a Challenge to recalibrate your life to the original intent of why God made you.** To calibrate means to measure according to the standard of excellence. With that in mind, how is your health? Are you physically fit? Do you have a regular exercise routine? What one thing could you do today to better your health?

Let's get moving. Let's recondition ourselves as if we are in training because we are. We're training to live the rest of our lives with purpose and on purpose, not wasting a single step.

PURPOSEFUL STEPS
- Get a physical.
- Define a healthy weight and body fat index.
- Join a gym.
- Hire a trainer.
- Start P90X.
- Set a challenge goal.

TODAY'S CHALLENGE
Set an appointment to get a physical, visit a gym, or order P90X.

DAY 1 • ADVENTUROUS SPIRIT

ACTION STEPS

....
....
....
....
....

NOTES • THOUGHTS • PRAYERS

....
....
....
....
....
....
....
....
....
....
....
....
....
....

IGNITE THE FLAME

> *"I remind you to fan into flame the gift of God that is within you."* 1 Timothy 1:6

The key to having life-long financial success is the realization that your greatest resource is the natural gift that is on deposit within you. God is wise enough to put reserves within His creation bountiful enough to sustain that creation.

The secret is digging deep to explore and discover your natural God-given abilities. It's time to start fanning into flame your gift.

START YOUR ENGINE
- Visit www.strengthsfinder.com.
- Make a list of your natural abilities.
- Ask trusted friends what they define as your natural gifts.
- Begin to sharpen your abilities.
- What problem does your gift solve?
- How can you monetize your gift?

TODAY'S CHALLENGE
Write down a list of at least five things you are gifted at doing.

ACTION STEPS

List at least five things you are gifted at doing.

....

....

....

....

....

Which one of these gifts brings you the most joy?

....

Which of these gifts come very natural to you?

....

Which of these gifts could be converted into additional income or a second job?

....

NOTES • THOUGHTS • PRAYERS

....

....

....

....

....

....

....

DRESS FOR SIGNIFICANCE

> *"When Pharaoh sent for Joseph, he was quickly brought from the dungeon. After he had shaved and changed his clothes, he entered the presence of Pharaoh." Genesis 41:14*

A gallant man is fashionable and groomed appropriately for every occasion. Men love to wear uniforms; some however have allowed their uniform to become sloppy and disheveled. If you were called into a very special meeting would you be embarrassed by your attire?

It's time for a man-makeover.

MAN UP YOUR WARDROBE AND APPEARANCE
- Visit a men's clothing store and gather ideas.
- Buy a men's style magazine.
- Get a new hairstyle and cut.
- Get a professional shave or beard trim.
- Trim your eyebrows, ear hairs, nose hairs, etc.
- Clean your closet.
- Donate clothes that are out of date.
- Buy three new outfits that coordinate.
- Buy new shoes and socks.
- Buy new underwear and sleepwear.

TODAY'S CHALLENGE
Start your man-makeover by cleaning your closet.

ACTION STEPS

....

....

....

....

....

NOTES • THOUGHTS • PRAYERS

....

....

....

....

....

....

....

....

....

....

....

....

....

....

WISE UP

> *"Proverbs… for attaining wisdom and discipline… for acquiring a disciplined and prudent life." – Proverbs 1:2*

As men, we have many responsibilities that require strong and decisive leadership. A good leader has great wisdom. Wisdom is the *knowing* and *applying* of principles for successful living. **The greatest pursuit of your life is obtaining wisdom.**

It's time to wise up. Commit yourself to gaining wisdom.

THE ULTIMATE PURSUIT
- Commit to reading one chapter of Proverbs each day for the rest of the Challenge.
- Read a biography of a successful man.
- Sit down with a man 10 years older than yourself and ask, "What advice would you give me if you were speaking to yourself ten years ago."
- Make the decision to be a reader.

TODAY'S CHALLENGE
Set aside 30 minutes to read. Consider making this a daily commitment.

DAY 4 • FAITHFUL IN CHARACTER

ACTION STEPS

....
....
....
....
....

NOTES • THOUGHTS • PRAYERS

....
....
....
....
....
....
....
....
....
....
....
....
....
....

BE A SOLUTION

"The Lord will reward everyone for whatever good he does." Ephesians 6:8

You were created to solve a problem. This speaks to the deep reservoir of purpose within you. Your life should be a contribution and not simply a withdrawal from other's resources. You must realize that you have been assigned to a particular problem.

Don't close your eyes and avoid problems. Rather, look for a problem that you are particularly created to solve. Take ownership of the problem and you will have the creativity to solve it.

"I never ask God to meet the need of someone when I have the ability to meet it myself." – Anonymous

SOLVE A PROBLEM
- It may be as simple as hanging a picture at your Grandmother's or Mother-in-law's house.
- It may be a need of someone in your neighborhood or church.
- It may be a total stranger (think of the Good Samaritan.)
- What do you have in your ability that someone else needs?

TODAY'S CHALLENGE
Don't end the day without meeting the need in someone's life.

DAY 5 • PHILANTHROPIC IN CAUSE

ACTION STEPS

....
....
....
....
....

NOTES • THOUGHTS • PRAYERS

....
....
....
....
....
....
....
....
....
....
....
....
....
....

BAD WEATHER PLAYER

> *"Whoever watches the wind will not plant; whoever looks at the clouds will not reap."* Ecclesiastes 11:4

You can't compete only on sunny days. **Don't allow circumstances beyond your control to control you.** You must be willing to condition yourself against the elements that resist you.

Don't excuse yourself. Get in the game.

DON'T EXCUSE YOURSELF
- Go play a game of basketball.
- Go to the driving range.
- Go to a shooting range.
- Play flag football.
- Join a rugby team.
- Try a hunting bow.
- Rent a boat for a day.
- Go fishing.
- Ride a bike.
- Rent a Harley.

TODAY'S CHALLENGE
Get moving – do something physical today!

DAY 6 • ADVENTUROUS SPIRIT

ACTION STEPS

....

....

....

....

....

NOTES • THOUGHTS • PRAYERS

....

....

....

....

....

....

....

....

....

....

....

....

....

....

DEFINE YOUR MISSION

> *"Come, let us build ourselves a city, with a tower that reaches to the heavens, so that we may make a name for ourselves." Genesis 11:4*

This is one of the best-formatted mission statements ever made. This statement is so precise that it involves clear communication to all people groups that were on the Earth at that time. It was so good that God commented, *"If as one people speaking the same language they have begun to do this, then nothing they plan to do will be impossible for them."*

A mission statement must be very clear to motivate a person to progress toward the stated goal. Most men will never take the time and energy to formulate a mission statement. It's one of the greatest mistakes we make as men.

It is similar to driving somewhere without knowing the directions. You simply won't get to your destination. We now have GPS systems for navigation. Think of your mission statement as a GPS system for your life. It keeps you on track.

LOCK IN THE COORDINATES
- **Identify Core Values:** Develop a list of attributes that you identify with.
- **Identify Your Calling:** With whom are you called to? Family, employer, friends, community, or the world.

cont.

DAY 7 • ENTREPRENEURIAL DRIVE

cont.

- **Identify Goals:** What is your highest priority in life? Write your goals, long-term and short-term. Start long-term first and then break those down into bite size pieces to define your short-term goals.
- **Write Your Mission Statement:** Based upon what you've identified previously, clearly define who you are and what you are about in a sentence or two.

My personal mission statement is: *To live proficiently in Biblical love, faith, health, and prosperity; to represent the foundational principles of wisdom by excelling in every area of life, leaving a legacy for my children's children.*

TODAY'S CHALLENGE
This challenge is hard. Write a mission statement.

ACTION STEP: MY MISSION STATEMENT

....

....

....

....

....

....

....

....

....

BE A BLESSING TO YOUR WIFE TODAY

> *"Joseph son of David, do not be afraid to take Mary home as your wife, because what is conceived in her is from the Holy Spirit." Matthew 1:20*

A husband should not view his wife as a burden, but as a blessing or a gift from the Lord. **God will never give you a gift meant to replace His presence in your life.** In the same way, you must realize that your wife has a personal relationship with God. She is not only your wife but she is also a spiritual sister in her own right. Her relationship with God is personal between her and Him.

Joseph was instructed to not enter into his relationship with Mary out of fear. Fear should never be the foundation of your marriage.

BLESS YOUR MARRIAGE
- Realize that God has ordained marriage.
- Maintain a passionate relationship in your marriage.
- Celebrate each other's personal achievements.
- You should desire to impress your wife; to live above her expectations.
- Share your goals and dreams. Be in agreement.
- Honor her relationship with the Father.

TODAY'S CHALLENGE
Purchase a card and write a personal note to your wife. Tell her how thankful you are that she is your wife and that she has a relationship with the Father.

DAY 8 • GALLANT IN RELATIONSHIPS

ACTION STEPS

....
....
....
....
....

NOTES • THOUGHTS • PRAYERS

....
....
....
....
....
....
....
....
....
....
....
....
....
....

THE AUTHENTIC MAN PRAYS

"Men ought always to pray, and not to faint." Luke 18:1

Prayer is a not a religious experience. It is foundational to the relationship between God and man. **Through prayer we have the ability to receive insight, instruction, and inspiration for successful living.**

Jesus taught us how to pray in Matthew 6:

- **Protocol & Paternal** – Our Father in heaven, Your Name is Holy.
- **Priority & Peace** – Your Kingdom come, Your Will be done.
- **Provision** – Give us today our daily bread.
- **Pardon** – Forgive us our debts, as we also have forgiven.
- **Protection & Power** – Deliver us from the evil one.
- **Praise** – For Yours is the Kingdom, Power, and Glory!

This simple outline gives you a complete overview of how to pray. I have prayed this outline for over 25 years. It works. The outline is a launching pad for my conversation with the Father. As you pray each part, expound on the topic. You will find yourself focusing on what you really need to communicate.

TODAY'S CHALLENGE
Find a secluded place to walk and pray this outline. Speak out-loud when you do.

DAY 9 • FAITHFUL IN CHARACTER

ACTION STEPS

....
....
....
....
....

NOTES • THOUGHTS • PRAYERS

....
....
....
....
....
....
....
....
....
....
....
....
....
....

HELP A STRANGER

> *"He went to him and bandaged his wounds, pouring on
> oil and wine. Then he put the man on his own donkey,
> brought him to an inn and took care of him." Luke 10:34*

We are never more like Christ than when we help a
stranger who is in trouble. **An authentic man has
compassion on those who are hurting.** Jesus taught the
parable of the Good Samaritan. This story has motivated
countless people to do good to strangers.

One day, I noticed a man standing on the side of the
road with a sign that read, "Homeless, please help. God
bless." I am ashamed to say that my initial thoughts were
very judgmental. Then I felt prompted to think, "Neil,
that is someone's son." I was immediately moved to do
something. I reached for my money clip when I saw that
all I had was a $20 bill. I paused for a second thinking,
"Man, I don't have anything smaller?" The light turned
green and I had to go, so I rolled down the window and
handed him the money. I spent the next few minutes
praying for him.

That experience challenged me to think of strangers as
neighbors.

TODAY'S CHALLENGE
Before you go to bed tonight look for a complete stranger
that you can help with a small gesture of money.

DAY 10 • PHILANTHROPIC IN CAUSE

ACTION STEPS

....
....
....
....
....

NOTES • THOUGHTS • PRAYERS

....
....
....
....
....
....
....
....
....
....
....
....
....
....

GET IN THE GAME

Jonathan said to his armor bearer, "Come on now, let's go across to these uncircumcised pagans. Perhaps God will work for us. There's no rule that says God can only deliver by using a big army. No one can stop God from saving when he sets his mind to it." 1 Samuel 14:6

Jonathan faced insurmountable odds, yet was willing to face the adversity of the challenge. **Sports challenge us to face the internal fears of competition, and the outward adversity of opposition draws out a deep river of spiritual adrenaline that translates into other arenas of our lives.**

It's time to get in the game. Pick a sport. It may be joining a softball team, basketball team, taking up golf, whatever you choose. Just get in the game!

"Sports remain a great metaphor for life's more difficult lessons. It was through athletics that many of us first came to understand that fear can be tamed; that on a team the whole is more than the sum of its parts; and that the ability to be heroic lies, to a surprising degree, within."
- S. Casey

TODAY'S CHALLENGE

Decide on a sport and get involved. Don't put this off – do it today!

DAY 11 • ADVENTUROUS SPIRIT

SPORTS CHECKLIST

- [ ] Softball/Baseball
- [ ] Golf
- [ ] Basketball
- [ ] Soccer
- [ ] Tennis
- [ ] Hunting
- [ ] Fishing
- [ ] Rugby
- [ ] Climbing
- [ ] Running

ACTION STEPS

....

....

....

....

....

NOTES • THOUGHTS • PRAYERS

....

....

....

....

....

....

....

....

ART OF WAR

> *"If the trumpet does not sound a clear call, who will get ready for battle?"* 1 Corinthians 14:8

Clarity is required for a successful strategy. If you cannot plan the next 24 hours, you cannot plan 24 years. Business can be best understood as economic warfare. **You must design a clear strategy for your business warfare.**

The United States Military has a manual for the art of warfare. Let's learn from it.

BATTLE STUDIES
- **Objective** – Clearly define the goal.
- **Offensive** – Initiate the strategy.
- **Mass** – Concentrate your efforts.
- **Economy of Force** – Allocate your resources.
- **Maneuver** – Obtain advantage over your opponent's weaknesses.
- **Unity of Command** – Make sure that you have the proper structure of leadership to ensure a win.
- **Security** – Never permit the enemy to acquire an unexpected advantage.
- **Surprise** – Don't forecast your moves to your opponents.
- **Simplicity** – Prepare clear and concise action steps to accomplish your goals.

TODAY'S CHALLENGE
Write a clear and concise strategy for your business. Even if you are employed by others, write as though it were your own.

DAY 12 • ENTREPRENEURIAL DRIVE

ACTION STEPS

....
....
....
....
....

NOTES • THOUGHTS • PRAYERS

....
....
....
....
....
....
....
....
....
....
....
....
....
....

STEWARD YOUR INFLUENCE

"A good reputation is more valuable than the most expensive perfume." Ecclesiastes 7:1

Most men do not steward their personal influence. You must recognize how important it is to develop and keep a good reputation. When you walk into a room, your personal presence is like a fragrance. If you have treated people in that room poorly you will be an odor to the room; however, if you have treated people well, it will be like a welcoming fragrance.

Influence is a currency. **Influence may be one of man's most valuable skills.** Solomon said, *"A good name is more desirable than great riches; to be esteemed is better than silver or gold."*

PURPOSEFUL STEPS
- **Dress for Respect** – Dress appropriately for every occasion.
- **Speak Clearly** – Pronounce your words clearly and fluently. Don't exaggerate an accent.
- **Use a Person's Name** – Repeat a person's name in conversation after you have met them for the first time so you can lock in their identity for later recall.
- **Avoid Jokes** – Very few jokes are worth repeating. Most are inappropriate. Natural humor is better than concocted humor.
- **Listen** – Give your ear to listening. Focus on the conversation that you are engaged in rather than eavesdropping on others.

cont.

cont.

- **Don't Grasp For Attention** – Our attitude should never be one to grasp for attention. It is beneath you as an authentic man to need the attention of the room. Don't raise your voice to be heard over others.

TODAY'S CHALLENGE

Have at least one conversation with a person whom you don't know very well. Learn their name, occupation, and where and how they were raised. Listen to their story.

ACTION STEPS

....

....

....

....

....

NOTES • THOUGHTS • PRAYERS

....

....

....

....

....

....

....

....

BOUNCE YOUR EYES

"Anyone who looks at a woman lustfully has already committed adultery with her in his heart." Mark 5:28

We cannot underestimate the destructive power of pornography. It is a scourge on society and is especially pathetic for men. Modern culture is so pervasive with sexual imagery that advertisers can't sell a hamburger without using it in their ad campaigns. It is a lazy strategy and an inexcusable insult to manhood.

You will never flourish in your personal relationship with your wife as long as you are divided in your affections with your eyes.

Learn to bounce your eyes away from attractive women. When you are watching television, learn to look away from the commercials that use sex to sell. When you are in a room and an attractive woman walks in turn away from her and do not gaze upon her.

The eyes are the gatekeepers to your thoughts. You can win this battle simply by developing the bounce technique. This is a real challenge but it is worth winning. You can do this! You can have a pure heart and life.

TODAY'S CHALLENGE

Go a full 24 hours without allowing your eyes to gaze upon a woman whether on television, websites, magazines, or in person.

DAY 14 • FAITHFUL IN CHARACTER

READ THESE SCRIPTURES

- [ ] Job 31:1
- [ ] Psalm 101:3
- [ ] Proverbs 22:14
- [ ] Matthew 5:27
- [ ] 1 Corinthians 6:18
- [ ] Colossians 3:5

ACTION STEPS

....
....
....
....
....

NOTES • THOUGHTS • PRAYERS

....
....
....
....
....
....
....
....
....
....
....

SOW A SEED

"Each man should give what he has decided in his heart to give, not reluctantly or under compulsion, for God loves a cheerful giver." 2 Corinthians 9:7

In the Bible, giving money is likened to sowing a seed as a farmer. A farmer knows that in order to have a harvest for his family that he must first sow a seed into the ground. A farmer also knows the quantity of the harvest is determined by the amount of seed that he sows.

We should approach giving financially as a farmer approaches sowing seed. Farmers do not reluctantly sow seed, nor do they flippantly scatter the seed. They are careful to sow the precious commodity into good soil.

The same is true for our giving. We should not approach giving without careful planning. Don't give out of compulsory persuasion, which means out of a guilt motivation. Our gifts should be expressed with clear joy and happiness that we are able to do so.

KEYS TO GIVING FINANCIALLY
- **A Confident Heart** – you feel very confident where you are giving.
- **A Considerate Heart** – you have examined what you are giving for and trust its worthiness.
- **A Heart of Gratitude** – you are able to express thankfulness while you are giving.

cont.

cont.
- **A Heart of Generosity** – you are willing to give in
  good measure without fear of loss.

Your gift is a seed that is sown into the lives of others. It
will produce a harvest.

TODAY'S CHALLENGE
Gather up all of your loose change. This is money that
you were not saving, investing, or using for your present
needs. Now, take it and sow it into a good cause. Express
joy by giving it because it was "worthless" to you before
but now it is "priceless" to your future.

ACTION STEPS

....
....
....
....
....

NOTES • THOUGHTS • PRAYERS

....
....
....
....
....
....

THE BULL RING

> *"Many bulls surround me; strong bulls of Bashan encircle me."* Psalm 22:12

As I mentioned in the book *FivestarMan: The Five Passions of Authentic Manhood*, I earned my place on the starting line-up on my freshman football team by proving myself in the "bull-ring" during a practice. **You may or may not know this, but you are surrounded by the enemies of authentic manhood.** It would be easy to simply give in and exile yourself into their ranks of effeminate, "culturally-relevant" man-boys but you would surrender your manhood doing so.

As C.S. Lewis said, *"Enemy-occupied territory – that is what this world is."* It is time we stand up and throw our shoulders back as men. It is time we face the challenge and be the man.

RECOGNIZE AUTHENTIC MAN'S ENEMY
- Manhood will always have an enemy. Living as an authentic man is counter-cultural.
- The enemy of manhood will attempt to redefine God's original intent for man.
- The enemy of manhood resents authentic man's desire to increase and be productive.
- The critic mocks the core values of authentic manhood as archaic and antiquated chauvinism.
- The critic will focus on the past more than understand the vision for authentic manhood.

cont.

cont.

The cultural attack against authentic manhood is so persuasive that we often don't recognize it. You are in a fight to be a man. Be strong and show yourself a man.

TODAY'S CHALLENGE

Listen carefully to news reports, carefully read articles, and discern the conversations around you to pick up on subtle destructive tones against authentic manhood. Write down a few examples of anti-manhood sentiment that you've heard.

ACTION STEPS

....

....

....

....

....

NOTES • THOUGHTS • PRAYERS

....

....

....

....

....

....

....

EXCEL IN BUSINESS

> *"Whatever your hand finds to do, do it with all your might."* Ecclesiastes 9:10

Most men want excellent lives with an 80 percent effort. **You will never gain the inertia of excellence without doing all that you can to do things better.** Excellence requires the extra 20 percent effort. The *Pareto Principle* teaches that the top 20 percent effort will produce 80 percent of the momentum. Very few businesses understand that this is what separates the great from the average.

If you are going to have a great business you must put in the extra effort to distinguish yourself from the average.

BUSINESS TIPS TO EXCELLING

- If you can – work from home. This will save you valuable time that is typically lost commuting to and from work.
- Create a rhythm of "you" time. I have learned to work in 15 or 30-minutes bursts of focus. This gives me undivided effort. I have also created a rhythm of days on and off work to help maintain my creativity.
- Take a real lunch break. Don't eat at the desk. Break away, get out in the weather, it will refresh you.
- Take calculated risks but don't bet the farm. To gain the inertia of excellence doesn't mean that we bet everything on one horse. We must push our teams to exert the extra effort that excellence requires.
- Excellence is in the details.

cont.

cont.

Once you have pushed through the barrier of excellence you will find that it is easier to get things done in the future. It is much like Roger Bannister breaking the 4-minute mile. Once Roger did it, hundreds have since made it common.

TODAY'S CHALLENGE

After performing a task today, reevaluate it with this question, "Can I do it better?" Find something that you can do better about that task and do it. This will begin a habit of pushing through the barrier of average.

ACTION STEPS

....

....

....

....

....

NOTES • THOUGHTS • PRAYERS

....

....

....

....

....

....

GENERATIONAL CONVERSATIONS

"Don't be harsh or impatient with an older man. Talk to him as you would your own father, and to the younger men as your brothers." 1 Timothy 5:1

As an authentic man, we should be very careful and respectful toward our relationships. We should show special honor toward older men. One key to doing so is hearing their story. Older men have a need to tell their story. We should take the time to listen. We should then turn and show attention to younger men. Young men need mentors. It is very important for us to develop this generational conversation - hearing the stories and dreams of the seasoned men - imparting wisdom for the vision of the younger men.

PURPOSEFUL STEPS
- Do you have a seasoned relative that you've not visited?
- Do you have an old mentor that you should look up again to have a conversation?
- Listen carefully to the older man's stories; you will pick up on amazing things that they were a part of in their lifetime.
- Don't ignore young men and don't assume that they know what you know.
- Teach young men practical things such as how to change a tire or keep a toolbox or tie a necktie. You would be amazed how many young men do not know how to do these things.

cont.

cont.

Let me give you a word of wisdom regarding the last tip; don't assume the role of a father. That is an awkward and inappropriate assumption. Be an elder brother in a young man's life.

It is very important that as we resurrect authentic manhood, that we establish proper relationships with other men.

TODAY'S CHALLENGE

Have a conversation with a seasoned man. Get him to tell you his story. Listen carefully.

ACTION STEPS

....

....

....

....

....

NOTES • THOUGHTS • PRAYERS

....

....

....

....

....

....

CONTROL YOUR TEMPER

> *"In your anger do not sin: Do not let the sun go down while you are still angry, and do not give the devil a foothold." Ephesians 4:26*

Do not allow the day to pass without ridding yourself of anger. Going to sleep while angry can cause a delusional mind. Our Nemesis will use anger to get a foothold on us through unchecked emotion. Anger digs deep into the soul of man. It can draw out buried emotion from years past in an instant. It is very important that we distinguish the different types of anger and extinguish the harmful emotions.

THE FOUR FACES OF ANGER

- **RAGE** is an anger that causes us to flurry about with over-expressed gestures, clinched jaws, or boisterous words, even calling down curses. This kind of anger typically comes from frustrated expectations. Expressing rage causes people around you to stare at you in disbelief, confusion, or embarrassment.
- **FURY** is a much stronger emotion of rage. It is a destructive form of rage often leading to a depraved mind and delusional violence. Fury is motivated by evil. This often results in physical harm to others, even murder.
- **INDIGNATION** is a righteous anger caused by witnessing or experiencing injustice, shame, or evil done to innocence. It is the correct use of the emotion of anger. Indignation motivates men to protect and risk our lives for the cause of others.

cont.

cont.
- **WRATH** is the Godliest form of anger. It is an anger that responds to evil with pure judgment. Wrath is what causes man to correct a wrong and to rid the earth of evil.

Some men have been taught to sequester their anger, to be stoic in emotions; yet anger has a role to play in our lives if our motivations are pure and our response is disciplined.

TODAY'S CHALLENGE
Resolve to properly manage any anger that you have today, not putting it off another day.

ACTION STEPS

....

....

....

....

....

NOTES • THOUGHTS • PRAYERS

....

....

....

....

....

....

INVEST IN A CHILD

> *"Defend the cause of the weak and fatherless; maintain the rights of the poor and oppressed."* Psalm 82:3

A philanthropic man is heroic in defense of the weak and the fatherless. We can do that by investing in children who are oppressed by systemic poverty.

My wife, Kay, and I have invested in the lives of children for more than 20 years. Our small monthly sponsorship transforms the lives of children by introducing them to the gospel, it pays for a quality education that empowers them to leave poverty behind, and shows compassion for their physical, health, and emotional needs as well.

Jesus said that what we do for a child is the equivalent of doing it for him personally. Can you imagine the privilege it would have been to be one of the wisemen who invested in the infant child Jesus? Yet, that is exactly what we are able to do when we invest in the lives of children.

TIPS FOR GIVING
- Know the recipient.
- Where will your money go?
- How much will actually get to the need of the child?
- Set goals for your giving.
- Give consistently.
- Make sure that you hear from the compassion ministry.

cont.

DAY 20 • PHILANTHROPIC IN CAUSE

cont.

If at all possible, take a trip to visit the ministry on the ground. I have found there are many scams out there. You must investigate the validity of the compassion ministry. I have found that LatinAmerica ChildCare is the overall best at what they do. You can reach them through **Fivestarman.com.**

TODAY'S CHALLENGE

Look into investing a few dollars every month into the lives of a child.

ACTION STEPS

....

....

....

....

....

NOTES • THOUGHTS • PRAYERS

....

....

....

....

....

....

....

THE SECRET PLACE

"Jesus, full of the Holy Spirit, returned from the Jordan and was led by the Spirit in the wilderness." Luke 4:1

There is a primitive call that resonates deep within the authentic man. **The Voice calls us into the wilderness for the experience of isolation.** Most men avoid it, they procrastinate answering the call, but once they do answer the summons they tend to experience something very profound. It is the wildness of their heart.

THE LESSONS OF THE SECRET PLACE

- Isolation is intimidating. It can expose your fears, insecurities, and weaknesses.
- Isolation is quiet. You begin to hear your spirit as loud as the sounds of a city in the middle of the day.
- Isolation is revealing. You begin to discern activity that is happening all around you.
- Isolation expands you. The expanse of the wilderness opens you up to new levels of faith.
- Isolation tests your character. When no one can see you, you expose who you really are.

Don't hide yourself in the crowd of activity. You need to get out in the wilderness and experience the powerful force of isolation. You will discover things about yourself that have been hidden. You will find yourself having open conversation with your Father. You will overcome your fears and find a new sense of security and strength of who you are.

cont.

DAY 21 • ADVENTUROUS SPIRIT

cont.

TODAY'S CHALLENGE
Find a place to get out into the wild. You may go camping or simply take a long hike up a mountain. Walk the banks of a river. Canoe a stream. Get alone.

ACTION STEPS

....

....

....

....

....

NOTES • THOUGHTS • PRAYERS

....

....

....

....

....

....

....

....

....

....

SET YOUR GOALS

"I press toward the mark for the prize of the high calling of God in Christ Jesus." Philippians 3:14

Mark McCormack in his book, **What They Don't Teach You In The Harvard Business School** tells of a Harvard study conducted between 1979 and 1989. In 1979, the graduates of the MBA program at Harvard were asked, "Have you set clear, written goals for your future and made plans to accomplish them?" It turned out that only 3% of the graduates had written goals and plans. 13% had goals, but they were not in writing. Fully 84% had no specific goals at all, aside from getting out of school and enjoying the summer.

Ten years later, in 1989, they interviewed the members of that class again. They found that the 3% of graduates who had clear, written goals when they left Harvard were earning, on average, ten times as much as the other 97% of graduates all together. The only difference between the groups was the clarity of the goals they had for themselves when they started out.

Establishing your goals is more than simply picturing a target, it is a process that starts from the end then develops back to the beginning. You actually begin with the end in mind.

FIVE MARKERS ON THE COURSE TOWARD GOALS
- **VISION:** The ability to visualize a desired future.
- **ACTION:** The activity that brings about an alteration by force.

cont.

cont.
- **ADJUSTMENTS:** The discernment to make necessary course corrections.
- **RESULTS:** To analyze the success of a determination.
- **PRUNING:** To cut off superfluous matter.

You will immediately establish yourself in an elite status if you are able to clearly define your goals. Doing so will empower you toward a new destiny.

TODAY'S CHALLENGE
Write out a list of 10 goals.

ACTION STEPS

....

....

....

....

....

NOTES • THOUGHTS • PRAYERS

....

....

....

....

....

....

WOMEN DESERVE YOUR RESPECT

> *"Treat older women as mothers, and younger women as sisters, with absolute purity." 1 Timothy 5:2*

A line of respect and familiarity governs every relationship. Crossing this line causes misconduct in the relationship. It is the principle of proximity. You cannot sin if you keep the proper relational distance.

A Fivestarman is gallant in relationships. Gallant means "to show special attention and respect toward woman in a honorable way." **The only woman who gets the intimacy of your eyes and the passion of your loins is your wife.** Job said, "I made a solemn pact with myself never to undress a girl with my eyes."

An authentic man should treat an older woman as if she is his own mother. We should treat younger women as if they are our daughters. We should treat our peers as our sisters. Doing so will not only protect us from inappropriate conduct but will sow seeds of protection for our own family members.

HOW TO TREAT A WOMAN WITH RESPECT
- Open the door for her.
- Stand up to greet her.
- Carry something for her.
- Keep at least two arms distance from her.
- Do not use crass language.
- Do not speak with harsh tones.

cont.

cont.
- Do not embrace her.
- Do not flirt with her.
- Do not communicate with her outside of proper protocols.

There are many ways this principle should be implemented into your life, especially with modern social networking. You must be very careful how you communicate with Facebook, Twitter, email, and texting.

TODAY'S CHALLENGE
During the day, look for ways to treat women with respect and give careful attention to them in an honorable way.

ACTION STEPS

....
....
....
....
....

NOTES · THOUGHTS · PRAYERS

....
....
....
....
....

TALK TO YOUR CHILDREN

> *"He will turn the hearts of the fathers to their children,
> and the hearts of the children to their fathers; or else I will
> come and strike the land with a curse." Malachi 4:5*

California State University reported that the average
father spends 3.5 minutes per week in meaningful
conversation with their children. **You cannot direct the
affairs of your children without having a relationship
with them.**

The Nemesis of mankind desires to deceive you by
convincing you that you have no role in the affairs of your
children. If he can't deceive you, he will distract you.
It is time for men to speak into the lives of their children
and direct them, instruct them, even command them in
the ways of God.

KEYS TO UNLOCKING CONVERSATION WITH YOUR CHILDREN

- Read the chapter of Proverbs that corresponds
  with the day of the month every day with your
  children. Proverbs is written as a "man-to-man"
  instruction book.
- Ask questions that require a thoughtful answer -
  something beyond "yes" and "no."
- Look into their eyes and listen carefully.
- Do not have your cell or computer in front of you
  while you are talking with your children.
- Turn the TV off.

cont.

cont.

- Play an old-fashioned board game or video game with your child.
- Have dinner together. Make everyone turn off his or her cell phones. No texting during your time together.
- Laugh. Laugh. Laugh.

The span of a childhood is only a few years. I remember the day I counted how many more summers I had with my children as teenagers. It made me slow down and focus upon them and less on me.

TODAY'S CHALLENGE
Spend an hour with your child or children doing something that they enjoy.

ACTION STEPS

....

....

....

....

....

NOTES • THOUGHTS • PRAYERS

....

....

....

....

BE KIND AND STAND FIRM

> *"Those who are kind benefit themselves, but the cruel bring ruin on themselves."* Proverbs 11:17

The word *philanthropic* means *the active effort to promote the welfare of mankind.* There are many "causes" today being argued and bandied about. **We must be able to kindly state our case and know what we stand for.**

As an authentic man, we should seek to calm the rhetoric of harsh and divisive arguments. Society has become increasingly hostile toward differing opinions. You've heard the statement that we can disagree without being disagreeable - and it's true.

Don't get me wrong. We must boldly stand up for what is right and against what is wrong. We must stand strong as men. We must stand upon principle and for liberty of man. However, we should look for the opportunity to live at peace with our fellow man even if we disagree.

HOW TO ARGUE YOUR CASE
- Don't argue for the sake of arguing.
- Know the subject.
- Support your cause with facts, you can't stand upon theories.
- Don't use personal attack to argue.
- Don't dismiss someone by claiming intellectual superiority.

cont.

cont.
- Concede on points that are true but stand firm upon principles.
- Don't use intimidating gestures and boastful tones.

If we believe in what we are doing we should be able to articulate it with passion.

TODAY'S CHALLENGE
Have a meaningful conversation with someone that has a different viewpoint than you do. Seek to find why they believe in what they are doing. This challenge can be deceptive. It may be harder than you think it will be.

ACTION STEPS

....

....

....

....

....

NOTES · THOUGHTS · PRAYERS

....

....

....

....

....

DON'T GIVE UP!

> *"Brethren, do not be weary in well-doing."*
> 2 Thessalonians 3:13

How is your fitness coming? Are you still focused? One of the challenges in moving forward is pushing through to the end. **The key is to not become weary in well-doing.**

To *weary* means *to become utterly spiritless.* Many times we can find ourselves worn-out trying to do better. At this stage of the challenge you may be questioning whether all this is worth it. This is the time to refocus on the goal. You may need to dig deep to tap into the adventurous spirit that resides within you.

You are drawing upon the uncommon reserves that men have but are often times unwilling to pursue. The adventurous spirit makes you get moving. It is easier to be comfortable, to simply settle for the status quo, but you will never reach your potential doing what is average.

The 45-Day Challenge is similar to developing strength through working out with weights.

KEYS TO STRENGTH BUILDING:
- **Resistance** is necessary because it strengthens your resolve.
- **Repetition** is important because it develops muscle memory.

cont.

cont.
- **Rest** is vital because it allows for recovery.
- **Routine** is mandatory because it develops habits.
- **Rewards** are celebrated because they motivate us.

Don't give up! Keep moving forward toward resurrected authentic manhood.

TODAY'S CHALLENGE
Refocus on your fitness. Check your weight. Check your routine. Are you coasting or are you pressing through? How is your diet?

ACTION STEPS

....

....

....

....

....

NOTES • THOUGHTS • PRAYERS

....

....

....

....

....

....

INTEGRITY IN BUSINESS

> *"But as for me, I shall walk in my integrity."* Psalm 26:11

The economic mess of 2008 was caused by the lack of one thing - a lack of integrity. Political maneuvering and an insatiable appetite of greed severed the thin line of integrity.

Integrity is foundational to having a long-term career or business. As the course is corrected, we should examine our relationships in business to make sure we are not allowing questionable partnerships to take root in our lives.

THE FIVE TESTS OF INTEGRITY
- Value **character** above talent.
- Value **self-control** above greed.
- Value **honest lips** above the flatterer.
- Value **diligence** above the zealous.
- Value an **honest assessment** over inflated books.

You are in business for the long haul not the get rich quick scheme. To have staying power we must operate our affairs with integrity.

TODAY'S CHALLENGE
Look over your business relationships. Do they pass the integrity test? Are you doing anything of questionable conduct? Be honest and evaluate your standing as a company or business.

DAY 27 • ENTREPRENEURIAL DRIVE

ACTION STEPS

....

....

....

....

....

NOTES • THOUGHTS • PRAYERS

....

....

....

....

....

....

....

....

....

....

....

....

....

....

HOW TO LOVE YOUR WIFE

> *"Husbands, love your wives, just as Christ also loved the church and gave Himself up for her."* Ephesians 5:25

Love is expressed in action. Consider how women have responded when asked to complete this sentence: "I wish my husband would love me by..."

- By listening to me.
- By taking my 'petty problems' seriously.
- By communicating more openly with me.
- By noticing me more – not just when he wants sex.
- By saying 'thank you' for the things I do.
- By being interested in my life – at least acting like you're interested.
- By showing affection when other people are around.
- By sharing his goals and values with me; talking his business over with me.
- By remembering me with little gifts or just planning an evening out.
- By taking me out without the kids more – maybe just for a ride.
- By including me in the things he does.
- By trying to understand me.
- By getting involved with things I enjoy doing.
- By just holding me in his arms and talking to me.
- By being tender and using kind, tender words.
- By helping in the discipline of the children.

cont.

cont.
- By saying little words of caring, compliments, and appreciation.
- By accepting me just as I am.
- By spending more time with the family.
- By making me feel like a woman.

TODAY'S CHALLENGE

Express your love toward your wife today in one of the preceding ways.

ACTION STEPS

....

....

....

....

....

NOTES • THOUGHTS • PRAYERS

....

....

....

....

....

....

....

....

WATCH OVER YOUR WORDS

> *"Simply let your 'Yes' be 'Yes,' and your 'No,' 'No';*
> *anything beyond this comes from the evil one."*
> Matthew 5:37

People have a tendency to exaggerate. You hear it when people want to emphasis something they habitually "over speak" such as, "I am sick and tired!" or "That's driving me crazy!" When describing something they look for the most current overused cliché. The vacuous person will often use expletive speech simply because they don't have the vocabulary to properly communicate, which reveals ignorance. Overspeak causes people to express extremes - their highs are really high - their lows are really low.

The Nemesis of man works in the gaps. He looks for ways to get into your life. The only way for him to do so is when we expose a gap. Between "Yes" and "No" is a gap. It's a gray area that allows Nemesis to work. Examine the attacks against your life. More than likely they are a result of a gap, a gray area, an exposed opening that was not defined by a simple "yes" or "no". Instead of exposing a gap we should mend the hedges, not leaving any room for doubt.

THINGS NOT TO SAY
- "I'm broke."
- "I'll never be able to afford it."
- "That's driving me crazy."
- "I am sick and tired."

cont.

cont.
- "You're killing me."
- "That breaks my heart."
- "I can't."

The key is to replace overspeak by minimizing the statement in a positive way. Doing so actually causes people to take notice even more of what you are saying. Not to mention the humor relief. The point is to watch over your words and say what you mean and mean what you say.

TODAY'S CHALLENGE
Offer family and friends $5 dollars for every time that you use overspeak or words that are pronouncements of sickness, financial lack, or even death over yourself.

ACTION STEPS

....

....

....

....

....

NOTES • THOUGHTS • PRAYERS

....

....

....

BLESSED TO GIVE

"It is more blessed to give than to receive." Acts 20:35

Researchers at the University of British Columbia found that spending on others boosted happiness and fulfillment while spending on one's self did not. (*LiveScience, March 20, 2008*)

It is a deep passion in our lives to do something of significance. Giving is foundational to who we are as men. We were created in the shadowed image of God; therefore, we take on and express his nature. God is a giver. In fact, He is the ultimate giver. *"For God so loved the world that He gave."* (*John 3:16*)

I believe we are the most like our Father when we are extending our hand toward the needs of other people.

Winston Churchill said, "We make a living by what we get, we make a life by what we give." As a Fivestarman, you have the entrepreneurial drive developing your personal gifts and accumulating resources. Your philanthropic passion balances out the greed factor. You defeat greed by motivating your passion to be philanthropic in cause.

GIVE YOURSELF AWAY
- **Give Financially** – Your finances represent you. It represents your time, energy, talents, skills, work, etc. Giving financially is the equivalent of giving of yourself.

cont.

cont.
- **Give Time** – Time is the most precious commodity that we have because we only have a limited amount.
- **Give Expertise** – Use your skill set to benefit someone who is in need of you.
- **Give Love** – The power of expressing love is immeasurable. It can be the difference of life and death for some.
- **Give Random Acts of Kindness** – This is an empowering way to give to others.
- **Give Appreciation** – It is very easy and very thoughtful to simply express your gratitude toward another person.

If you truly want to be a blessed man, you must learn that you are blessed to be a blessing.

TODAY'S CHALLENGE
From the list above see how many ways you can give yourself away today.

ACTION STEPS

....

....

....

....

....

BE A MENTOR

> *"These things happened to them as examples and were written down as warnings for us, on whom the fulfillment of the ages has come."* 1 Corinthians 10:11

When you are a player, you need a coach. A coach helps draw out the skills that are within you.

Even champions need a coach.

Solomon said, "When the ax is dull, more skill is required." You must sharpen yourself and your efforts to be a winner. Developing a winner mentality is not done so that you become boastful and obnoxious. Rather that you may be the best at your game and draft others to new levels of competition as well.

KEYS TO GREAT COACHING
- Know the game.
- Practice the fundamentals.
- Conditioning yourself for the game.
- Improve your skills.
- Discipline your emotions.
- Keep your head in the game.
- Pre-play your game. You have the ability to simulate conditions of the game.
- Know that team play always trumps individual play.
- Keep it simple.

cont.

cont.
Players are empowered by the confidence and poise of
a coach.

Games and sports serve as examples to help translate the
skills we master on the field of contest into the field of life.
Developing these skills will help you reach new levels in life.

TODAY'S CHALLENGE
Rent a movie with the storyline of a coach and player
relationship. Look for the key lesson that is told in the
story. How can you apply that into your life?

ACTION STEPS

....

....

....

....

....

NOTES • THOUGHTS • PRAYERS

....

....

....

....

....

....

BE A SALESMAN

"Through patience a ruler can be persuaded, and a gentle tongue can break a bone." Proverbs 25:15

Every man needs to be able to close a deal. You may or may not earn your living as a salesman but you still need to have a sales technique in your toolbox. Many people fear the close of the deal. It is the moment of decision. It can be awkward if you are not convinced that you are offering a mutual benefit in the exchange.

6 KEYS TO CLOSING THE SALE
- Always let the other prospect have his say. Don't interrupt.
- Repeat and acknowledge any objection before resolving the objection.
- Be pleasant, agreeable and receptive to objections without argument.
- Don't assume the other person knows what you know about your product or service.
- Don't assume that your prospect needs your product or service.
- You will never make the sell without a win-win proposition.

Sales are as basic to business as you can get. As David Green, the founder of Hobby Lobby said, "The core activity is buying and selling merchandise."

TODAY'S CHALLENGE
Sell something! Even if you are not in the business of sales – find something in your possession to make an exchange.

DAY 32 • ENTREPRENEURIAL DRIVE

ACTION STEPS

....

....

....

....

....

NOTES • THOUGHTS • PRAYERS

....

....

....

....

....

....

....

....

....

....

....

....

....

....

THE FRIEND VIRUS

"Avoid godless chatter, because those who indulge in it will become more and more ungodly." 2 Timothy 2:16

Surveying the nations top lawyers reveals more and more clients are filing for divorce as a result of behavior on social networking sites. Social networking is not the cause of inappropriate behavior - it simply exposes it.

The Bible warns that we should avoid godless chatter, which means that **we should refrain from empty discussions, useless conversations, or discussion of vanity.** Social networking can be a very positive tool and bring constructive results if we are careful in its use. At the same time, it can reveal and destroy your life if you are overexposed to it.

SOCIAL NETWORKING RULES
- Keep your private life private.
- Don't play meaningless games.
- Too Much Information (TMI) is destructive.
- Unfriend a person who has inappropriate conversations.
- Don't participate in live chats with unknown people, particularly with the opposite sex.
- Don't say anything that is inappropriate to say face to face.
- Don't get pulled into the drama of another person's life.
- Delete your account if necessary.

Social networking can be a positive thing if you approach it properly. Knowing that whatever you say and do on these sites

cont.

cont.
are public record will help you make wise decisions
whether or not to post your comments.

TODAY'S CHALLENGE
Review your personal use of social networking. Are you
conducting yourself properly?

ACTION STEPS

....

....

....

....

....

NOTES · THOUGHTS · PRAYERS

....

....

....

....

....

....

....

....

....

....

THE DEVIL IS A GAMBLER

> *"The thief, if he is caught, must pay back double."*
> *Exodus 22:7*

Jesus said, "The thief cometh not, but for to steal, and to kill, and to destroy." One of the great principles in spiritual warfare with man's nemesis is **when a thief is caught he must pay back a double portion.**

This is good news if you know how to fight to win. If you're facing challenges and opposition, make no mistake about it; the fight is for your possessions, for your family, and for your life. We're not gaming here! It is real. If you don't understand this, you will lose it all.

However, if you stand firm in your faithfulness, if you do not waiver in unbelief, and if you do not compromise your integrity, you will win. By doing so you are literally resisting the devil and he will flee from you.

There are two extremes that defeat most men:
1. You *under*-estimate the devil's deceptive powers, or
2. You *over*-estimate his powers.
Either choice puts you at the disadvantage.

Jesus taught us through his temptation in the wilderness how to man-handle the devil.

cont.

cont.
KEYS TO WINNING THE DOUBLE
- **KNOW WHO YOU ARE:** Be authentic to God's original intent for you. Have your identity sealed. Satan bluffed, "If you are the Son of God." Jesus refused to forfeit his identity for a loaf of bread.
- **KEEP YOUR FOOTING:** Satan bluffed, "cast yourself down." Our enemy will always try to trip us up. The steps of a righteous man are order of the Lord.
- **STAY FOCUSED:** Finally, Satan proposed, "All of this I will give you." By showing Jesus the splendors of this world, he was offering the world without sacrifice. You will never gain through compromise.

Jesus was faithful to defeat the devil. The devil left him, awaiting another opportunity.

TODAY'S CHALLENGE
Read Matthew 4:1-11. Are you gambling with your identity? How secure is your footing? Are you focused on where you are going?

ACTION STEPS

....

....

....

....

....

....

GIVING GOALS

"So let each one give as he purposes in his heart."
2 Corinthians 9:7

As authentic men, we understand that we are motivated to meet the needs of our lives, supply the needs of family, and even grant the desires of their hearts. This represents the heart of God for that is how He thinks as well. We are also motivated to finance our purposes.

Recently, I was with a Fivestarman entrepreneur who is investing a great deal of his resources into worthy causes. He made this statement, "Neil, I don't have income goals, I have giving goals."

What do you have in your heart to do? What cause would move you so passionately that you would sacrificially give toward it?

One billionaire told me, "It is no longer about whether or not we need another store to open. The question has become, "If we open another store, how much more money would that allow us to give to our causes?"

By focusing your life goals on giving, you will tap into the greatest power known to man and that is true purpose for living.

TODAY'S CHALLENGE
Write a list of 10 giving goals.

DAY 35 • PHILANTHROPIC IN CAUSE

ACTION STEPS

....
....
....
....
....

NOTES • THOUGHTS • PRAYERS

....
....
....
....
....
....
....
....
....
....
....
....
....

DON'T WASTE A CRISIS

> *"There went out a champion out of the camp of the Philistines, named Goliath." 1 Samuel 17:4*

John F. Kennedy said, "Khrushchev reminds me of the tiger hunter who has picked a place on the wall to hang the tiger's skin long before he has caught the tiger. This tiger has other ideas." **Giants are opportunities that cause the weak to flee and the bold to arise.**

THREE REWARDS FOR FACING GIANT CHALLENGES
Great Wealth
- Your rewards are in direct proportion to solving problems.
- Look for problems that others are ignoring.
- Look for residual pay for problems solved today.
- You will never become rich while remaining comfortable.
- The only difference between your future and the present is the challenges that you are willing to face.

Special Status
- Influence is a greater currency than money.
- Influence is not fame. Fame is fleeting. Influence is legendary.
- Influence is a key that opens great doors of opportunity.
- Influence ushers you into a room of great men.

cont.

cont.

Royal Lineage

- A decision today can affect your descendents forever.
- Stepping up to the challenge can redirect your future.
- The prophecies and promises of your childhood will be revealed on the field of contest.

When you step onto the field of contest, resist the fear of the challenge; you will reveal the anointing that lies deep within your manhood. Be strong! Show yourself a man.

TODAY'S CHALLENGE

Look for a problem. Identify it. Think about it. How can this be solved? Is it something that can be made to return a residual income? Find a problem today.

ACTION STEPS

....

....

....

....

....

NOTES · THOUGHTS · PRAYERS

....

....

....

....

A STRATEGIC IDEA

> *"In breeding season I once had a dream in which I looked up and saw that the male goats mating with the flock were streaked, speckled or spotted." Genesis 31:10*

Jacob was working for a schemer, a man who repeatedly changed his wages every time that Jacob began to prosper. Yet, Jacob had a very unique dream. This idea also came with a detailed strategy; which is the key to financial increase.

An idea is worth a dollar; a strategy is worth a million dollars. If you get an idea, you must process it.

STEPS TO PROCESS AN IDEA
- Be curious.
- Find a problem.
- Write it down.
- Test it.
- Protect it.
- Network it.

One idea can give you an income the rest of your life. If you have an income problem, dream again. Things do not just happen. Things are made to happen.

TODAY'S CHALLENGE
Conceive and process a strategic idea.

DAY 37 • ENTREPRENEURIAL DRIVE

ACTION STEPS

....

....

....

....

....

NOTES • THOUGHTS • PRAYERS

....

....

....

....

....

....

....

....

....

....

....

....

....

....

INTENTIONALLY DATE YOUR WIFE

> *"All night long on my bed I looked for the one my heart loves; I looked for him but did not find him."*
> *Song of Solomon 3:1*

We should continue to court our wives as if we were still trying to win their affection. Keep the spark in your marriage alive by making it a practice to take your wife out on dates. Make it an intentional date; meaning, don't get in the car and say, "Where do you want to go?" Plan ahead as if you were courting her.

A princess likes to be rescued. A date can rescue your wife from the mundane habits of her life. The excitement of dating never leaves the deep passion of a woman. Keep it alive in your wife. It's better for you in the long run.

DATE TIPS FOR THE MARRIED MAN
- Prep yourself. Dress in upscale casual clothes. Ditch the every day jeans and teeshirt.
- Make reservations. Go for a nice restaurant with an upscale ambiance.
- Don't be cheap. This is a time to invest in your marriage. You are showing appreciation for her and what she means to you.
- Set the date and time. Let her know well in advance and keep the commitment.
- Hire a baby-sitter. It is preferable for the children to stay overnight with a grandparent so that you can have the whole night to yourselves.

cont.

cont.

- Consider a resort or luxury hotel. You can get luxury hotels very inexpensively on bargain websites.
- Send her gift certificates to prepare for the date. Perhaps a gift certificate for shopping clothes or nightwear. Consider gifting a manicure and pedicure.
- Send her a gift to be delivered on the afternoon of your date such as flowers or simply a hand-written card telling her that you are anticipating the night.
- Make sure your car is spotless!
- Open doors for her.
- Be a gentleman.
- Stay focused on her. Don't talk about the kids, work, or problems. Reflect upon your meeting and dating. Talk about your future together.
- Laugh.
- Laugh. I know I repeated this but it is important. It is good medicine.

TODAY'S CHALLENGE
Make a date with your wife.

ACTION STEPS

....

....

....

....

....

DO WHAT YOU SAY

> *"Someone will say, 'You have faith; I have deeds.' Show me your faith without deeds, and I will show you my faith by what I do." James 2:18*

The Bible speaks of "clouds without rain." You know men who are always promising but never delivering - they are indeed clouds without rain. To be authentic means that we must do what we say. You can constantly affirm something but without the discipline to do it you are living a delusion.

Steve Jobs said, "Some people aren't used to an environment where excellence is expected." You will set yourself apart from mediocrity the moment you decide to follow through and finish well. In fact, you will never gain the inertia of momentum until you become a doer of your words.

The same is true for your faith walk with God. There are men who give their walk with God a casual stroll. Your walk with God should have your foremost effort. It should be vibrant and alive, brisk and quick. It should get your juices flowing. Doing so will take you to a new level of living.

12 KEYS TO BEING AN AUTHENTIC MAN
- To be a man of order – pick up after yourself.
- To be a man of integrity – don't lie.
- To be a man of discipline – exercise daily.
- To be a man of wealth – manage your money.
- To be a prudent man – keep a secret.

cont.

cont.
- To be a man of wisdom – listen.
- To be a man of knowledge – read.
- To be a man of passion – live.
- To be a man of adventure – get moving.
- To be an attractive man – take care of yourself.
- To a man who speaks well – articulate your words.
- To be a successful man – love, because it never fails.

The story of your life can be rewritten. I suggest that you leave out the drama and live the adventure. You can redefine yourself in a moment but you will prove it over a lifetime.

TODAY'S CHALLENGE

Make a change in whom you are. Say out loud that you are the kind of person that you want to become. Now that you've said it – repeat it – and live it out.

ACTION STEPS

....

....

....

....

....

....

....

BE REMEMBERED

> *"Store up for yourselves treasures in heaven, where moth and rust do not destroy, and where thieves do not break in and steal." Matthew 6:20*

In the last season of a man's life his mind begins an internal audit. He will ask himself the question, *"Did I do anything of significance? Will I be remembered?"*

You can spend your life accumulating things - we certainly have a lot of stuff available to us. You can christen your boat with your name and sail off into the sunset. You may even name a foundation after yourself and give all of your money away. Whatever the case, you will only have significance in what is eternal. Everything is else is summed up in Solomon's conclusion, "Everything is vanity."

Only that which is invested in the living is eternal and only man will live eternally. This earth will pass away. Only man will step out of this life and into the eternal realm. At the core of our activity on earth is the reality that we will only be remembered by the people who share our story.

At the very heart of the philanthropic man is being significant. Significance is much greater than success. Jesus said, "moth and rust destroy, thieves steal." It is all meaninglessness if we do not invest in the eternal.

cont.

cont.
As Leroy Landhuis said, "We're all going to die, and you want to make sure you've invested your life wisely."

KEYS TO ETERNAL GIVING
- Start small.
- Invest regularly.
- Investigate the charity.
- Invest smartly.
- Make sure that the money solves a systemic problem.
- Invest more in people than in buildings.
- Evaluate your giving regularly.
- Keep a relationship with the recipient organization.
- Keep a giving journal.
- Don't just do it for tax benefits.

TODAY'S CHALLENGE
Give something to someone today.

ACTION STEPS

....

....

....

....

....

NOTES • THOUGHTS • PRAYERS

....

....

THE FIELD OF CONTEST CALLS YOU!

Within every man is a spirit of adventure. It is who you are and how you are made. You were sculptured from the clay and it is where you relate to other men. Men relate shoulder-to-shoulder facing challenges. The Bible says that men sharpen one another as iron sharpens iron. You are sharpened not by the caress but by the clash with other men.

On the field of contest, you are challenged to dig deep, to fight through fears, to exercise aching muscles, and to face your opposition. The risk is something that calls for you – it summons you to the dual.

Come on! Get up and face it. Get dirty. Risk the injury. Will you get hurt? Maybe. Will you learn something about yourself? Absolutely!

TODAY'S CHALLENGE
Schedule a real adventure!

DAY 41 • ADVENTUROUS SPIRIT

ACTION STEPS

....

....

....

....

....

NOTES • THOUGHTS • PRAYERS

....

....

....

....

....

....

....

....

....

....

....

....

....

MAKE SOME MONEY!

Within you lies a deep reservoir of wealth. It isn't out there somewhere to discover, it is within you. God created you in His shadowed image. That means that you have a deposit of resources that await your discovery.

You do not have to be nomadic – going from job to job looking for your income. You can dig deep and draw upon your God-given gifts to meet your needs, satisfy your wants, and fund your purpose.

Now... do something brilliant. Discover. Cultivate. Sharpen your skill set. Others will flock to pour money into your lap to purchase your gift.

TODAY'S CHALLENGE
Start a business!

DAY 42 • ENTREPRENEURIAL DRIVE

ACTION STEPS

....

....

....

....

....

NOTES • THOUGHTS • PRAYERS

....

....

....

....

....

....

....

....

....

....

....

....

....

LIVE THE LOVE LIFE!

No man can be authentic without expressing love in his relationships. You are the source of love for your family. They need to not only hear you say it but also see you express it.

A gallant man is honorable in his relationships. He relates to women who are older as his mother. He honors a young woman has his own daughter. He treats his peers as his sister. The only woman who gets the intimacy of his eyes and the passion of his loins is his wife.

A man who loves his wife and children will not do anything to bring harm to his family.

DO NOT SURRENDER YOUR DIGNITY by being dishonorable.

TODAY'S CHALLENGE
Tell your family that you love them.

DAY 43 • GALLANT IN RELATIONSHIPS

ACTION STEPS

....

....

....

....

....

NOTES • THOUGHTS • PRAYERS

....

....

....

....

....

....

....

....

....

....

....

....

....

BE A MAN OF FAITH!

The authentic man is spiritual without being religious. He is practical in his faith, not pious. He has integrity in his character. He is authentic to his call to be a man.

Your Father created you for a personal relationship with Him. That relationship is not liturgical or ritualistic but it is revealed in the daily commute. As you walk with Him, you will grow more and more like Him. The Bible says, "He who walks with the wise grows wise."

TODAY'S CHALLENGE

Purpose in your heart to completely and passionately become a man of faith!

ACTION STEPS

....

....

....

....

....

NOTES • THOUGHTS • PRAYERS

....

....

....

....

....

....

....

....

....

....

....

....

....

....

LIVE A LEGACY!

You are here for a short time. It is not important to know when you are going to die; it is important to know when are you going to live.

You can spend your days chasing the wind – things that you simply can't grasp. You can drive the cars, wear the clothes and live in the cottages. The reality is at the end of your life you will look back and be disgusted with it. You will die a miserable old man embittered by life.

Or you can live a legacy. You can do something of eternal significance. You can make a difference in this world. You can be remembered.

TODAY'S CHALLENGE

Do something today that will be remembered!

DAY 45 • PHILANTHROPIC IN CAUSE

ACTION STEPS

....
....
....
....
....

NOTES • THOUGHTS • PRAYERS

....
....
....
....
....
....
....
....
....
....
....
....
....
....

• •

During the last few days of the 45-Day Challenge I have summarized the things you have learned regarding authentic manhood.

By completing the 45-Day Challenge, I believe you have set your life on a course for greatness and that you have made lasting and eternal changes. I believe that you are conditioning yourself to be the authentic man that God originally intended for you to be.

I would like to personally invite you to communicate with me. Go to our website at fivestarman.com and tell me your story.

I look forward to hearing from you today.

Let's work together to resurrect authentic manhood in our time!

-Neil Kennedy

• •